CRAZEMAN IN THE BOTTLE

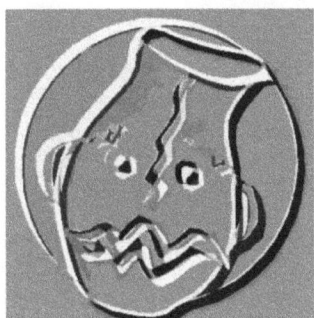

Sally Stiles

CRAZEMAN IN THE BOTTLE

Sally Stiles

Pale Horse Books

ISBN 978-1-939917-10-2

Printed in the United States of America
April, 2014

Pale Horse Books

www.palehorsebooks.com

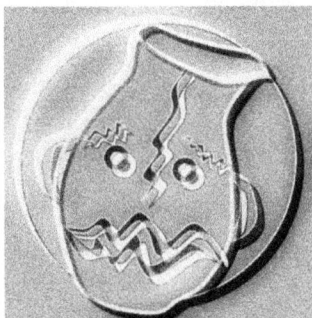

In memory of David—
so much poetry

This refrain
my brain keeps humming,
a multitude of messy tunes
seeking true timbre.

Table of Contents:

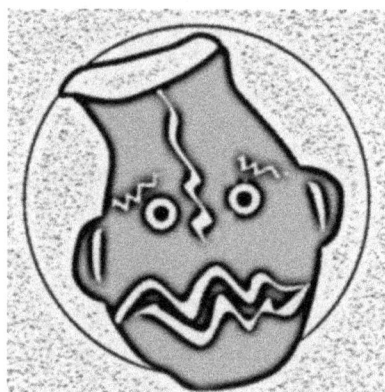

Moments of Grace

I once came close enough
to taste the stars,
the peppermint, the lime.
My toenails were shapely, thin,

my charm bracelet heavy
with moments of grace.
Forgiveness grows a child.
I'm only granted

a single poem, evolving title to title,
form to form, quartz crystals
glinting in unpolished stone,
sweet puppies rolling

off my tongue.
Moments of recrimination
to moments of grace.
Again. Again.

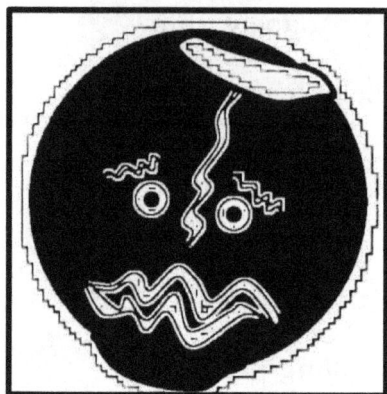

Old Spice

"Old Spice smells like old men."
"Old people don't smell so good" – Internet Posts

Kenny smelled of Bazooka and hickory nuts
filched from neighborhood lawns.

Saturdays at the Roxy, Commando Cody
zipped his rocket-powered flying suit

and Kenny shouted "Bombs over Tokyo!"
as Martians assaulted the earth.
                    Zombies of the Stratosphere 1952

Egyptian frescoes, velvet swags and lofty
private boxes at Peachtree Street's Lowes Grand

where I fell in love with foreigners as handsome
and hazy as my dad. Becky, Betsy and I

tittered at boys one row down
who fondled us with smoke from their Lucky Strikes.
                    Three Coins in the Fountain 1953

We starched our petticoats, sprayed Dior
on our ears and wrists, rushed to the front

to stake our claim on Ashley Wilkes.
Others waited patiently at the *Coloreds Only* door.
                    Gone with the Wind Revival 1954

Ted reeked of Old Spice, garlic and sweat.
His fresh crew cut inched closer every reel.
Sayonara 1957

Protestants didn't date Catholics.
Only Jews befriended Jews.

To Presbyterians, Southern Baptists were suspect,
full immersion a probable sin.

Blacks lived somewhere out of sight.
Asians and Greeks were tolerated

for their restaurants.
Phil was safe, an Episcopalian

who smelled of tetrazzini and angel food
served at St. Luke's family suppers.

In the balcony, I pulled my hand from his
and shut my eyes at Darlin' Jill, naked in the tub.
God's Little Acre 1958

When Bobby and I trolled the Varsity in his green
MG, my classmates strained to look indifferent.

The carhop brought frosted shakes, chili cheese dogs
and fried peach pies. Bobby tapped his pipe

and reached across the shifter with his Phi Delt pin
wrapped in a whiff of Cherry Blend.
Psycho 1960

At The Purity we swigged pitchers of 3.2 beer,
rewrote *Franny & Zoey, Coney Island of the Mind.*

Tom was English Leather, a lathered stallion rolling
in lush moss. All films worth seeing were foreign.
Jules et Jim 1962
8 ½ 1963

Patrick's hair shimmered below his old tweed cap.
A man preferring him to me followed the scent

of Brylcreem all the way from Julius,
the bar still coming out, to Christopher Street's

subway stop. At Penn Station I sprang the train
and waved them off toward Times Square.
A Hard Day's Night 1964

Felix stank of turpentine, cadmium blue.
All women were works of art. All love was free.
I am Curious (Yellow) 1969

Alan surfaced from musk and anise,
the aura of Brut, the smell of money.
The Great Gatsy 1974

The scent of David was David,
at times mixed with a little hairspray.

The Spy Who Loved Me 1977
E.T. 1982
Driving Miss Daisy 1989
Schindler's List 1993
Forrest Gump 1994
Saving Private Ryan 1998
A Beautiful Mind 2001
Hotel Rwanda 2004
Slumdog Millionaire 2008
The Kings Speech 2010

He slipped away before the credits ended.
I still have the shirt he wore—

a trace of sea salt, cedar shavings, puppy fur,
polished loafers, lantern light,

eucalyptus pulp, Johnnie Walker Black,
The Selected Poems of Robert Frost,

a beat-up Stetson, Remington oil,
dahlias on a hillside and mussels in white wine.

Pegasus winked

"To be or not to be an adventurer
who dares step out on her own...."
—Phyllis Barber, *Raw Edges*

She buried her veil
under her mother's pearls,
locked the box,
hid temple garments beneath black sox,
painted her legs blue denim.
She wrapped a bottle of Beaujolais
in a scarf to match her dust-blue eyes,
floored the Corvette onto I-89.

Between the prophet's birthplace
and Three Penny Tap
she rolled back the top,
turned up the heat,
sniffed the air for transfigurations.
She sped past dreary gods
comatose in the milky way.
Pegasus was grazing on gamma rays.

She squealed to a stop,
stroked the soft tip of his nose.
Pegasus winked.
She quivered with rapture
and trepidation,

hopped on his back,
grabbed his mane.
They raced solar winds,
pursued the night
beyond an endless black hole
where she dazzled
in new church clothes.

Absolution

You vanished inside
your virtual Saloon
while I twirled the world
on tiptoe, barely touching ground.
I sent you a dozen letters,
became an only child.

I splashed alone
through Mother's tears,
trod nimbly over Father's faults,
assembled a volume
from yellowed scraps
then climbed your cybernetic steps
and held my breath
beneath the crosshead.

I pushed aside the slatted door,
strode across the sawdust.
You held my book as gingerly
as Mother's brittle Bible,
dipped a finger in absolution
and carefully turned each page.

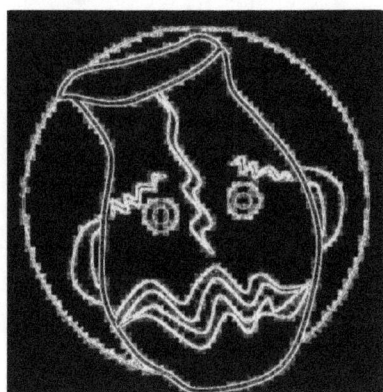

Cornish, NH

I want to travel slowly
against the river,
cross the oldest wooden bridge,
listen for the welcoming clap
of tires on joins,
pass St. Gaudens' bas relief,
regiment fifty-four
marching to the Civil War,
the ghosts of nonchalant picnics,
stately hollyhocks
on a patriotic day.
I want to dawdle

at the gristmill by the Blow-Me-Down,
read to the water's beat
of plowmen, fences, woodpiles, roads
not taken. I want to pinch sea salt
from a loaf still warm,
the butcher block still dusted
with King Arthur flour.
Our too-tall mansard
on a clapboard box,
the ugliest house in New Hampshire,
New Jersey French Provincial
you always said.
Damn! It's for sale. You and I
had so many houses, so few homes.
I want to throw

the garage door open;
strap on skis in our back yard,
make a run
to the sheltering oak
on Maxfield Parrish's lawn—
purples and oranges leaping from
his palette to stain the sky.
Come spring I want to stand

on our listing deck,
watch the river hurling ice,
sleep under Mount Ascutney's shield
knowing you will soon arrive
from Mgololo, Myanmar, Timbuktu.
I want to write more

than a poem permits about the mountains
and the flats, the ancient scent of pine,
your Pendleton plaid, Mad River canoe.
Forty-two square miles,
seven hundred houses,
a private game preserve,
the ragged stones across the road where all
our grandfathers lie.
I want to walk

our then-loved dogs,
Murray, the noble shepherd,
the deaf, contented mutt JR,
and stop for an hour
in Rose's canning kitchen,
smell cucumbers
pickling in sharp brine.
I want to tell his fans

that Holden Caulfield's dad
lived among the maples,
his unassertive pine chalet
a turn beyond the Burling's
hunting-season sign: *Don't Shoot
the Horses.* I want to write

the truths Salinger sought.
Living there, in his shade,
so hungry after six fallow years,
I filled so many pages
I pretended it was I
eluding capricious fame.
I want to immortalize

this town: the murderers, suicides,
poets, tax dodgers, devout Catholics
and pious agnostics, clever professors,
blueberry pickers, tree tappers.
Those who host stylish dinners,
exhibit pumpkins at the Cornish fair. I want

one more quiet twilight,
sun hovering over a river,
moon rising fast,
the two of us dipping paddles home.

The Successful Poet

*For the students in CRWR 470,
William & Mary, 2014*

Tonight I almost googled
how to be a successful poet,
as if I didn't know:
tenacity, precision, tempo,
an extravagant soul.
A poet mines the unfathomable,
digs with baby spoons,
selects fine sable brushes
to sweep away debris.

No poet writes for money,
love, a hope of being understood.
They write to give what's not forthcoming
from a lover across a breakfast nook,
a companion on a slow train ride.

A poet doesn't respond
to a poet: *you have no right.*
Or *I skipped to the end.*
Or *way too deep.*
Or *maybe I'll borrow a copy.*
A poet says *thank you,*
and that is all
a poet needs to hear.

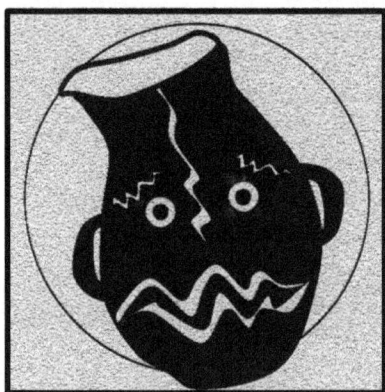

Last Words

She walked 94 years
until her toes
bent down and under.
She wanted no more
than one more chance
to dance, even if ever so slowly.
Lisa strapped on the gait belt,
raised her to the parallels.
One foot high,
then the other. We sought
an exultant smile, instead
her stubborn eyes, determined chin.
Lisa held the belt higher.
I trailed with the chair
across the room, step
after dogged step,
until she collapsed
in a teary *thank you.*

In the dining room
Miquel arose, walked
to the cupboard
and with only the slightest quiver
braced himself against
her table, laid a clean bib
across her chest, kissed
the top of her head:
You are truly beautiful woman!

She hugged herself
with a smile, and as I turned
away, the last words
I ever heard her say
to all who ever placed
a tender hand on her shoulder:
Thank you. Everyone is so kind.

Twenty One

I stuff the furrows of my brain
into my safe deposit box,
head for the pub,
two double bulls, a triple
twenty, Sam Adams cold
and quenching.
I flirt with a hundred
possibilities,
kiss off failure,
blow despair.
I'm the twenty-one
I never was,
my brain from birth deeply etched
by generations fearing hell.

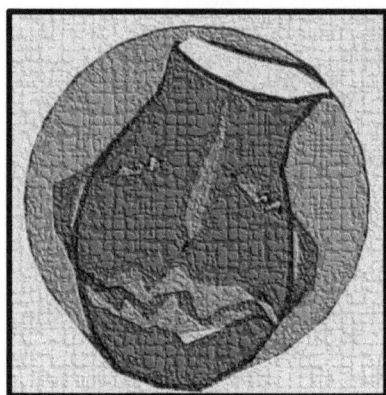

The gift of Cheetah

For Sudi Kombo (1952-1994)

"There were coffins everywhere."—Ted Conover,
Trucking through the AIDS Belt,
The New Yorker, August 16, 1993

Sudi wasn't afraid
to say he was afraid of lions.
He could spot a lion half a klick away.
Mufindi to Iringa to Dar,
Mikumi, Moshi, Zanzibar.
Two years of rutted roads
churning up dust, laughter and lions.
Our final trek to Dar
Sudi slowed the car,
gave me the gift of cheetah.

Sudi was already thinning.
I bought him potatoes, beef and beer,
and for his wife Indian cotton,
magenta, gold, black,
and toy Ferraris for the twins.
Because she cried when I held her
I bought his little Aziza the only
mzungu doll in the market, eyes blazing
blue, the left askew. Crouched
in her solitary bed, Aziza clutched
that doll and whispered:
"She is not afraid."

The cheetah stopped short, yellow eyes
scanning the car, posed for a dozen
shutter clicks then vanished
into the sisal.

Sudi smiled at me, stepped on the gas,
his Timex swinging loose on his wrist,
the awful proof. For Sudi, Aziza,
hundreds more clutching at time
from a solitary cot in Arusha, Dodoma, Dar,
no *mzungu* could ever buy
any damn thing that mattered.

Mama Yetu

You spilled from cement block,
corrugated tin,
blue shorts creased,
white shirts tenderly re-mended.
A sun-spotted river,
three hundred children,
for a moment, mine.

You settled on the dirt,
whispering until
Hafsa's voice, silvery-green,
as astonishing as first leaves in spring,
began to sing: *mama yetu, our mother.*

A dozen more voices,
sweet counterpoint,
mama yetu, our mother,
we will never forget you,

our mother, thank you.
our mother, safe journey.

When I search my life
for treasure you still sing
to me. Your voices linger over a schoolyard
dusty with looming drought,
a schoolyard stripped of all I left undone.

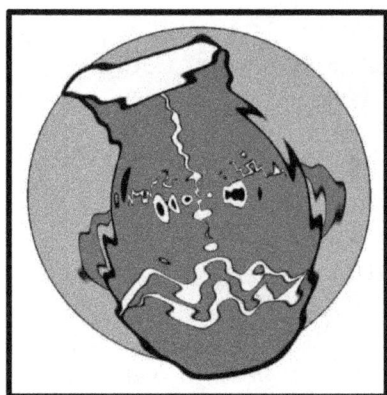

Hamad's Petrol Station

The Arabic toilets
at Hamad's Petrol Station
aren't fit for shit,
but I gotta go.
In the truck
driver, cook, union leader
shouldn't see me pee
on some baobab tree
down the road.

At Hamad's Petrol Station
a parrot lands
on a three-legged table,
grabs a boney wing
from a boney driver;
a one-eyed cat
leaps on the table,
claws the air,
misses the parrot.
The driver swipes at the cat.

Fat Hamad from
his wire mesh window
shouts at the driver,
not at the parrot,
not at the cat.

At Hamad's Petrol Station
boycooks fry samosas,
chicken and chips
in old gnu.
Pepsis are hot
as pavement tar.
I haven't eaten
since breakfast in Dar.
A Pepsi and English biscuits,
on the shelf
two rainy seasons,
down the Arabic toilet

at Hamad's Petrol Station
where company drivers receive
a thousand shillings
over pump price,
enough largesse
for two warm Tuskers
at Hamad's Petrol Station.

By three o'clock
Hamad fills
his new Land Rover,
leaves for Iringa,
his plaster palace,
three young wives,
eleven children,
eleven gold-plated bathrooms
all with sit-down toilets.

Market Child

Don't run from me.
Listen, this is true:
the ochre bones
of our common story
lie deep below
these wooden stalls.
You extend saffron hands,
ask for candy. Your uncle
sells me nougats,
keeps the change,
scratches a tumor
big as an onion on his jaw.
I give you nougats,
only nougats. I want.
You want. So much more.

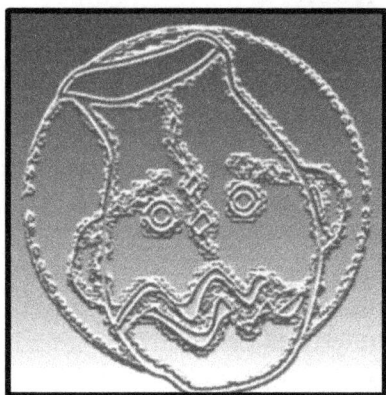

Grief

The mourners stumble
through the maize,
a moving impasto of purples and blues.
The only sound the squish of mud
under plastic sandals.

One who prayed in church this morning
wipes the ashes from her brow,
ponders why the priest refused
to drive Dafina home, why the doctor
sent away a blood-stained woman,
why missions from America
donate medicine he sells.

The women shift their babies higher,
slide kanghas over trusting eyes,
bow their heads as they pass
the dented white pickup truck,
the raw pine box bearing both
the unborn child and Dafina,
just twenty-one, too soon returning
to her mother's village.

They approach Obediah,
murmur *pole sana.*
From each bosom the fifty shilling note
saved for next week's coal, tomatoes.
Their hands reach out to hold his grief.
He whispers a stunned *asante sana.*

The women huddle by the eucalyptus.
No song can reach their tongues.
One by one they embrace,
and when their voices carry
on the evening wind,
a low moan trembles across the valley.

Baba Yetu

Outside my window
night voices impatient
like the wind.
I pull the curtain,
test the bolt, pray:
Our father,
baba yetu, uliye mbinguni.
Hallowed be thy name.
A sudden hush.

Night breezes
brush the scarp,
tease with my screen door.
A gecko slithers
across my floor.
Bare feet make no noise.
Is that a click? *Deliver us*
from fear.

Who would hear my cries?
A hundred thousand crickets?
A mosquito jabbing
a sleeping child?
A python at my door?
Ufalme Wako Uje.
Thy kingdom come.

The Makonde in the market
rubs shoe polish on his carving,
erasing white streaks
from Blackwood. How I long
to knead Africa into my skin.

In the simmering city
I have seen bold women caper
with bamboo juice, dance
with spirits I have long ignored.
Are they ghosts of shared beginnings?
Deliver us from fear.

There but for grace I walk five miles
across the Iringa valley,
a jug of water on my head,
bowing to my husband:
Bwana, may I have twenty shillings,
a mango for the baby?
What is that noise?

Mzungu stripped the forest
of monkeys, mambas, ebony,
planted dreary tea.
My Land Rover narrows the distance
between what I need and desire.
I keep my rings in dark boxes
so they don't glitter. You own, Lord.
We merely borrow
a scrap of time, of land.
Only bare feet can feel the land.

Baba yetu, uliye mbinguni,
Jina lako litukuzwe.

Who lingers outside my window?
Are your pangas honed sharp
like sawgrass? When you cut
through my whiteness will you find
my blackness? *Baba Yetu.* I pray.

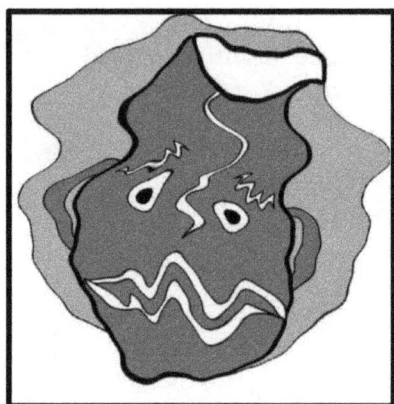

Some Day I'll Sell My Potatoes

Some day the juju son
of God will float down Kilimanjaro,
kneel before me,
shine like the Ruvu River
on a yellow day. Oh, yes.
He'll shine golden-golden
and sing in the sweet one voice
of many children.

Slowly, so slowly
he'll slip his hand
from his gleaming ghalabayeh,
bless my potatoes, each one.
He'll turn up his palm,

star his crown with my potatoes.
They'll shine like tears. Oh, yes,
they'll shine. He'll slide
his sparkling fingers
over mine and fly away.
My hand will be thick
with silver shillings.

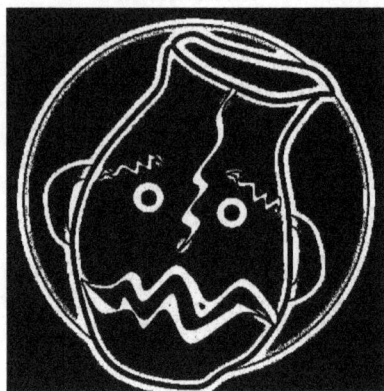

Dust

One eye open, lion sleeping.
Mama, can you hear me weeping?

I have no goat for Ramadan.
A pocket full of dust.

Pink rat prowling Zanzibar.
Mama, can you hear me weeping?

Children's bellies fat with hunger.
A pocket full of dust.

One eye open, white man sleeping.
Mama, can you hear me weeping?

A pocket full of dust.
Mama, can you hear me weeping?

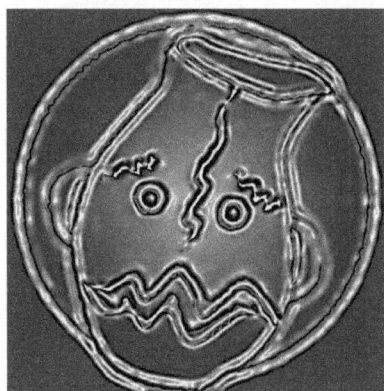

Rain

The sun sips up the Kiamba River. Small threads of water trickle through cracked, red mud. Two elephants dig in their tusks, squirt droplets in a newborn's mouth. Samwell watches the elephants wander downriver, thrusts his gourd into the mud, looks up at the sky, questions the Great Mother:

"I've outlived my wife and three children. Will I now die from lack of drink?"

Two more days, nights without rain. Samwell wakes to hear his curtain slapping across the door, thunder roaring like a distant lion. He runs outside. Black clouds lope across the mountains.

"Rain!" He laughs. "Rain!

Samwell opens his mouth to welcome first drops, lays his gourd against a stone, watches it fill as if he's never met rain in his eighty-three years. Raindrops bounce as high as his knee. He dances a stiff *kwasa-kwasa*, savors meals to follow: mounds of *ugali*, fat papayas, curried fish.

"Thank you Great Mother."

The Kiamba river begins to boil like *Mtori* on a furious fire. Muddy water whirls through the papyrus, swallows a pine sapling, a bridge. Baobab limbs hurtle down river, a fleet of dhows gone berserk.

"Stop, Great Mother! Stop!"

Samwell's straw roof collapses. He digs up his pot of dry maize kernels, stuffs his pants pockets full. An ancient pine, wrenched from the soil, moves like a spirit through the backwater, stumbles. Roots flail in the air. The Great Mother flicks her thumb, tosses up a chimney pipe, a goat, the hood of a car. Samwell cries out:

"Enough, Great Mother! Enough!"

Muddy water slaps at Samwell's feet, upsets his cook pot, steals his gourd. He slips down the bank on slick red clay, grabs a young acacia, hangs on with both hands. The Great Mother punches the river, churns it until it foams. Samwell loses his grip, spins downstream. Water fills his nostrils, his throat. He sinks into the river, rises again. A dozen lizard buzzards fly overhead.

"Save me, Great Mother!" he whispers.

The Great Mother raises Samwell from the river, strokes his hair, rocks him in the cradle of her palm. She carries him across the savannah, past the mangrove swamp to the sandy shore. Without a word she releases him to his ancestors deep within the sea.

Shaman

He leans on twisted staff,
climbs red dirt roads,
rustles tattered doors,
his mouth so bittersweet
he might be tasting truth.

His folded face, riddled beard,
eyes that see more
than eyes can see:
earthen pot, banyan tree, barefoot boy,
the glimmer of possibility,
the afterglow.

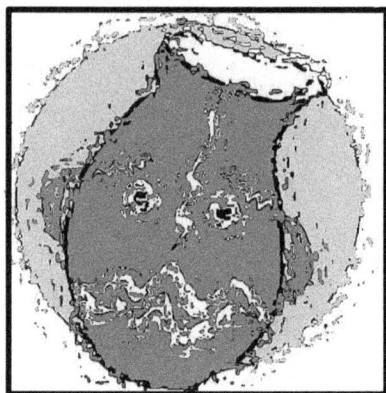

Joy to the World

Eda and Helen
knock cautiously—
Upendo comes timidly

from the garden. We bake
stiff gingerbread Josephs,
manger pigs and chickens,

sing *Joy to the World*
off key in two languages,
roll more dough.

Through the week we braid
gold wreathes of frangipani
swags of pine, eucalyptus,

float gossamer orchids
in plastic tubs, revel
in iced lime sodas,

breaded eggplant,
bowls of cool whipped cream,
melting chocolate,

teach each other Christmas.
Eda wedges a pine branch
in a water pot. We dress it

to kill: rhinestone earrings,
painted dough, one red sock,
wrapping paper.

We sing *Oh, Come All Ye Faithful.*
Helen blesses the tree.
On day three

they knock boldly,
on day five, walk right in
singing *Joy to the World—*

Furaha Kwa Ulimwengu—
as if singing makes it true.
We lavish cakes

with pink and turquoise
icing, lettuce leaves,
hibiscus, candied cherries,

excess in the name
of Christmas.
There is nothing else

to overdo. We step outside
into the glow of Mgololo's sun,
Bethlehem's sun,

take cakes and kilo sacks
of clean white rice
to village Christians,

Muslims, sing *Mjini Bethlehemu*
house to house,
crossing time and place,

close now to the manger,
almost close enough to sing
Joy to the World.

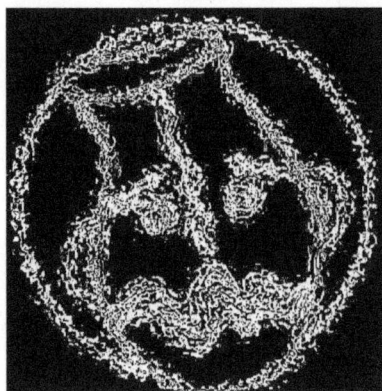

The Piki-Piki

For Headmistress Helen Nkanda

Brown kanga fluttering
over brown ankle, Helen rides
her piki-piki home from school.

It skitters a rut, chickens squawk,
blue books scatter,
children run from their shambas,

push the piki-piki
through Helen's gate,
her front door, where it squats,

chrome-dazzzle, strawberry red,
between her two-burner cooker
and low slat bed.

Through the night the piki-piki flies
Helen from dream to dream.
Her mother and father

live again. Her sons have grown
into caps and gowns, stroll
with their children through London.

In the morning she refills the tank,
resolves her way down
the saw-edged road to school.

Crazeman in the Bottle

From a calabash
as big as the moon
Obatala filled his jug.

He'd designed so many animals:
eyes, feet, lungs, veins,
gastric systems, sex organs

he was bored.
Another jug of ogogoro,
another scheme.

He'd never made a zebra
willing to shackle brothers
of a darker stripe,

a schizoid leopard,
an insurgent rhino,
a degenerate giraffe.

He'd never known
a double-crossing kudu,
a hypocritical lion.

Vipers and tigers would tremble
before his new creations
existing as they chose.

Obatala worked all night,
drank the calabash dry,
named his masterpieces man.

He invited them to play Mancala.
The insurgent made a slingshot
to launch the playing stones.

The degenerate pilfered the board.
Obatala flung them all
across emerging jungles, belched and went to bed.

Ogogoro is a fermented wine distilled from the juice of
the raffia palm. It is known by many names, including
craze man in the bottle.

Swahili translations:

Asante Sana: Thank you very much.
Baba yetu, uliye mbinguni, Jina lako litukuzwe. Ufalme Wako Uje:
Our father which art in heaven, may your holy name be honored. Thy Kingdom come. (Note: spellings and words are not the same in every translation of the Lord's prayer.)
Khangas: strips of cloth used as wraps for skirts and tops.
Kwasa-Kwasa: a fast dance with the hips moving back and forth.
Makonde: an ethnic group in southeast Tanzania and northern Mozambique known for their wood carvings.
Mancala: an African board game where stones are moved from cup to cup.
Mgololo: a town in the Iringa district of Tanzania.
Mtori: stew.
Mzungu: a foreigner, an outsider or white person.
Piki-Piki: motor scooter.
Pole Sana: so very sorry.
Shamba: farm.
Ugali: a cornmeal porridge.

Yoruba creation myth: In the beginning there was only sky above and water below. Obatala procured a long gold chain, a snail shell filled with sand, a white hen and palm nut. He climbed down the chain. When he reached the end, he poured out the sand and released his white hen. The hen scattered the sand, forming hills and valleys.

Obatala dug a hole and planted his palm nut. It grew immediately into a tall tree, dropping nuts which grew to more mature trees. He wanted company, so dug into the sand, found mud and fashioned new beings. When he grew tired, he stopped and made wine from the palm trees and drank many bowls. Then he went back to making beings out of mud. He asked the chief god Olorun to breathe life into his creatures. When they came alive, he was horrified to discover the imperfections of those he had made while drunk on palm wine.

Dust is loosely based
on a Bantu response work song,
no doubt the antecedent to slave work songs.
Responses are based on intuition more than logic.

This Refrain, Market Child and *Shaman*
appeared in a similar form in *Plunge!,*
a memoir by Sally Stiles.

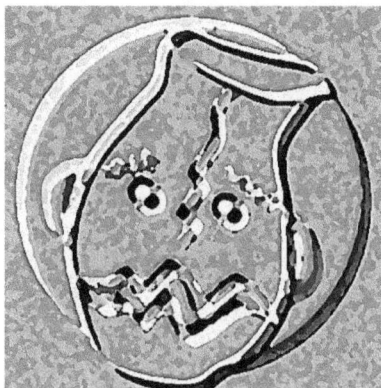

With gratitude to Henry Hart,
the students in CRWR 470,
The College of William & Mary, 2014.
Also Kit Fournier, John Conlee, Patricia Gray,
Dalia Liddiard, Carol Lynn Marrazzo.

Back cover photo by Betty Schelley.

www.ingramcontent.com/pod-product-compliance
Lightning Source LLC
Chambersburg PA
CBHW021223020426
42331CB00003B/450